DATE DUE			
3-25-98			
4-15-98			
5-29-98			
FE 15 '02			

92
MIL

Thornley, Stew.

Sports great Reggie Miller

SPORTS GREAT REGGIE MILLER

—*Sports Great Books* —

Sports Great Jim Abbott
(ISBN 0-89490-395-0)

Sports Great Troy Aikman
(ISBN 0-89490-593-7)

Sports Great Charles Barkley
(ISBN 0-89490-386-1)

Sports Great Larry Bird
(ISBN 0-89490-368-3)

Sports Great Barry Bonds
(ISBN 0-89490-595-3)

Sports Great Bobby Bonilla
(ISBN 0-89490-417-5)

Sports Great Roger Clemens
(ISBN 0-89490-284-9)

Sports Great John Elway
(ISBN 0-89490-282-2)

Sports Great Patrick Ewing
(ISBN 0-89490-369-1)

Sports Great Steffi Graf
(ISBN 0-89490-597-X)

Sports Great Wayne Gretzky
(ISBN 0-89490-757-3)

Sports Great Orel Hershiser
(ISBN 0-89490-389-6)

Sports Great Bo Jackson
(ISBN 0-89490-281-4)

**Sports Great Magic Johnson
(Revised and Expanded)**
(ISBN 0-89490-348-9)

Sports Great Michael Jordan
(ISBN 0-89490-370-5)

Sports Great Jim Kelly
(ISBN 0-89490-670-4)

Sports Great Mario Lemieux
(ISBN 0-89490-596-1)

Sports Great Karl Malone
(ISBN 0-89490-599-6)

Sports Great Reggie Miller
(ISBN 0-89490-874-X)

Sports Great Joe Montana
(ISBN 0-89490-371-3)

Sports Great Hakeem Olajuwon
(ISBN 0-89490-372-1)

Sports Great Shaquille O'Neal
(ISBN 0-89490-594-5)

Sports Great Kirby Puckett
(ISBN 0-89490-392-6)

Sports Great Jerry Rice
(ISBN 0-89490-419-1)

Sports Great Cal Ripken, Jr.
(ISBN 0-89490-387-X)

Sports Great David Robinson
(ISBN 0-89490-373-X)

Sports Great Dennis Rodman
(ISBN 0-89490-759-X)

Sports Great Nolan Ryan
(ISBN 0-89490-394-2)

Sports Great Pete Sampras
(ISBN 0-89490-756-5)

Sports Great Barry Sanders
(ISBN 0-89490-418-3)

Sports Great John Stockton
(ISBN 0-89490-598-8)

Sports Great Darryl Strawberry
(ISBN 0-89490-291-1)

Sports Great Isiah Thomas
(ISBN 0-89490-374-8)

Sports Great Herschel Walker
(ISBN 0-89490-207-5)

SPORTS GREAT
REGGIE
MILLER

Stew Thornley

—Sports Great Books—

ENSLOW PUBLISHERS, INC.

44 Fadem Road	P.O. Box 38
Box 699	Aldershot
Springfield, N.J. 07081	Hants GU12 6BP
U.S.A.	U.K.

Library of Congress Cataloging-in-Publication Data

Thornley, Stew.
     Sports great Reggie Miller / Stew Thornley
     p. cm. —(Sports great books)
     Includes index.
     Summary: Describes the personal life and basketball career
of the tough-talking shooting guard for the Indiana Pacers.
     ISBN 0-89490-874-X
     1. Miller, Reggie, 1965- —Juvenile literature. 2. Basketball players—
United States—Biography—Juvenile literature. [1. Miller, Reggie, 1965- .
2. Basketball players. 3. Afro-Americans—Biography.] I. Title. II. Series.
GV884.M556T56   1996
796.323'092—dc20
[B]
                                 95-51447
                                     CIP
                                     AC

Printed in the United States of America

10 9 8 7 6 5 4 3 2 1

Photo Credits: Frank P. McGrath, pp. 36, 43, 54; R.L.P. 1995, pp. 9, 11, 13, 17,
19, 39, 47, 50, 57; UCLA Sports Information Department, pp. 26, 29, 32;
University of Southern California, p. 22.

Cover Photo: R.L.P. 1995

Contents

Chapter 1

Only one quarter remained in the fifth game of the 1993 National Basketball Association (NBA) Eastern Conference playoff series. Whoever won this game between the Indiana Pacers and the New York Knicks, at Madison Square Garden in New York City, would need only one more win to advance to the NBA Finals against the Western Conference champion. At this point, things didn't look good for the Pacers. After three quarters, the Knicks had built a 70–58 lead.

Reggie Miller, the Pacers' ace shooting guard, seemed to have lost his shooting touch. Although he scored fourteen points, he made just six of the sixteen field goals he attempted. "But it was a good six for 16," he said later. "It seemed like every one of my misses had gone in and out." Obviously, his confidence wasn't shaken, and he added, "I made a decision that I was going to shoot us right back in the game or shoot us right out of it."

In the opening minute of the final quarter, the Pacers took off on a fast break. Indiana's Kenny Williams set a screen to block out defenders. Reggie Miller made the most of the clear shot his teammate was providing, getting the ball and throwing up a long shot, long enough that it was worth three points when the ball sailed through the basket. The Knicks responded with two points of their own, but it was the last scoring New York would be doing for a while.

Back downcourt, Miller took a pass from Williams, set up in the left corner, and buried another three-pointer. When Kenny Williams followed with a jumper to cut the New York lead to six points, Knicks' coach Pat Riley called time out, hoping to stop the Pacers' momentum. It didn't work.

Reggie Miller got the ball and drove into the free-throw lane. He pulled up, faked one shot to get his defender off balance, then fired a fifteen-footer that was good. Although the Knicks were still clinging to a lead, Miller's performance was taking its toll on them. "Every shot that Reggie made in the fourth quarter was like a bolt of lightning to the Knicks, leaving them shocked, stunned, almost paralyzed," wrote Clifton Brown in *The New York Times* the next day.

Reggie Miller was shooting the Pacers back into the game, which was just fine with his teammates. They've come to depend on Miller for his leadership, his flair, and most of all, his skills as one of the premier shooting guards in the league.

The two guards on a team's backcourt have different roles. The position Reggie Miller plays is known as the shooting guard (sometimes called the off guard) to distinguish it from point guard. While a point guard is relied upon for running the offense and passing the ball to the big men inside, it's the shooting guard's job to light up the scoreboard. Few would argue that the greatest shooting guard in the history of basketball is Michael Jordan of the Chicago Bulls. Jordan stepped away from basketball between 1993 and 1995, and during his absence a poll was taken of NBA players. They

During the Eastern Conference playoffs, Reggie Miller knew that he had to shoot the Pacers back into the game. His skill helped the Pacers come back from a 70–58 Knick lead.

were asked to name the best shooting guard currently playing in the league. They chose Reggie Miller.

One of Miller's trademarks is his deadly jump shot. Another is his mouth. In a sport with its share of "trash talkers," players who try to get in the face of an opponent and intimidate him with tough talk, Reggie Miller stands out.

In this playoff game in New York, though, he has some competition when it comes to trash talk. Strangely, it's not from the Knicks but from one of their fans, filmmaker Spike Lee. Lee, who is known for taunting opposing players, is sitting courtside and has been doing his share of yelling at Reggie Miller.

However, Miller manages to silence Lee; and he does it without even saying a word. After sinking a twenty-foot jump shot that puts the Pacers within two, at 72–70, Miller looks at Lee and puts both his hands around his throat. The gesture is clear. "The Knicks are choking," Miller is telling the filmmaker. Lee has no comeback, perhaps because he knows Miller is right.

The Pacers tie the game on a pair of free throws by Haywoode Workman. It's not tied for long, though, as Reggie Miller launches a twenty-six-footer from the top of the key. His third three-pointer of the quarter puts the Pacers ahead, 75–72.

The Knicks finally score to break the fourteen-point run by Indiana, but Miller comes right back with two more three-pointers, making him five-for-five in the quarter from long range.

Before he's done, he adds another two-point basket, along with four free throws down the stretch. Reggie Miller finishes the game with 39 points, 25 in the final period, to carry the Pacers to a 93–86 victory.

Some observers said that this was more than a sensational shooting exhibition. They said that in the fourth quarter,

Reggie Miller has silenced critics like Spike Lee with his consistently outstanding performances.

Reggie Miller seemed to be in an altered state, or "in a zone" as it is called when a player is so focused that he seems to be performing unconsciously. Miller himself said it was like the game was being played in slow motion during that final period. "I saw players cutting *before* they cut. I knew things were going to happen *before* they happened."

Unfortunately for Reggie Miller and the Pacers, the Knicks went on to win the final two games to capture the playoff series and advance to the NBA Finals.

Even so, it was still Miller's performance that had fans talking—in Indiana, in New York, and throughout the league. For his sharpshooting—and his even sharper jousting with Spike Lee—Reggie Miller ended up as a guest on David Letterman's late-night television show and soon made the rounds on all the big talk shows.

Ever since he was chosen as the top draft pick of the Indiana Pacers in 1987, Reggie Miller has been the center of attention in Indianapolis, but that one quarter of basketball in New York elevated Miller to national stardom.

Teammate Byron Scott summed it up by saying, "What you saw was Reggie stepping up to the next level."

In a way, Reggie was doing more than just stepping up. He was also stepping out—out of the shadow of his older sister, Cheryl. Cheryl Miller is considered by many to be the greatest women's basketball player of all time.

Cheryl Miller made headlines in high school when, on more than one occasion, she slam-dunked the basketball—a feat unheard of for women. By the time she was in college, Cheryl was the subject of feature articles in national magazines such as *Sports Illustrated*.

Reggie never minded the attention his sister received. He and Cheryl are best friends; each is the other's biggest fan.

The final quarter in the fifth game against the Knicks in the Eastern
Conference playoffs elevated Miller to national stardom.

They helped one another become better as they squared off in one-on-one games while growing up.

But opposing fans have used Cheryl as a way of taunting Reggie. When he would go to the free-throw line, fans would chant, "Cher-yl, Cher-yl," as a way of saying that Reggie wasn't even as good as his sister. Reggie Miller's father referred to it as the fans "giving him the Cheryl." Probably because of the closeness between him and his sister, Reggie Miller claimed the chants didn't bother him. "When people yell her name," he said, "that's an orchestra to me." On the other hand, he freely admits that having a famous sister has created some challenges, and once said, "Overcoming my sister's shadow has been the biggest obstacle of my life."

Although she's enjoyed the spotlight, Cheryl Miller was more than happy to see her brother recognized for his accomplishments, not hers. Referring to his 1993 heroics that pushed the Indiana-New York playoff series to the limit, Cheryl said, "Taking the Knicks to Game Seven really boosted Reggie's confidence. Now he knows he's a superstar."

For Reggie Miller, his great performance against the Knicks was part of a continuing saga of memorable moments in New York. It was in the same city eight years before that Reggie's college team, the UCLA Bruins, won the National Invitational Tournament.

As it turned out, Reggie Miller was still just setting the stage for more heroics in Madison Square Garden. New York fans had not seen the last of Reggie Miller.

Chapter 2

Someone once asked Saul Miller, Sr., if he knew how talented his son Reggie was. "It was hard to say," replied Saul, "because of all the talent that surrounded him."

When Reggie was born on August 24, 1965, to Saul and Carrie Miller, he already had three older siblings. Eventually, he would be joined by another sister.

Saul's comment about talent refers to his entire family; talents ranging from sports to music.

Saul himself provided a great deal of the family talent. In his hometown of Memphis, Tennessee, he was a high school All-American in basketball. He carried his court skills into college, where he made the All-Conference team. But Saul had an even greater love than sports. He was a fine saxophone player and performed in a number of jazz bands.

He played with such legends as B. B. King, Ike Turner, and Lionel Hampton and was an original member of the Phineas Newborn quartet. While playing in jazz bands in California, Saul joined the Air Force. When his four-year commitment was over, he returned to Memphis. Saul's sister was in nursing school, and she had a classmate she wanted her brother to meet. That classmate turned out to be Saul's future wife and the mother of the talented clan.

Soon after Saul and Carrie Miller were married, Saul rejoined the Air Force. While his primary work in his next twenty-one years in the military was with computer systems, Saul still found plenty of time for his music. He finally retired from the service in 1977, holding the rank of Chief Master Sergeant, and transferred his computer skills to a medical center in Riverside, California. Carrie Miller continued her medical training and became a registered nurse.

All five of the Miller children were born while their father was in the Air Force. The oldest, Saul, Jr., was born in Memphis before the family began relocating, a normal part of life in the military. A second son, Darrell, was born in Washington, D. C. The other three kids—Cheryl, Reggie, and Tammy—were born in Riverside, California, when their father was stationed at nearby March Air Force Base.

Saul, Jr., followed in his father's footsteps in two ways: music and the military. Saul plays in the Airmen of Note, the premier jazz band of the Air Force. Darrell blazed the way for the Miller children in sports. He played a number of sports as he grew up, but finally settled on baseball and had a five-year major-league baseball career as a catcher and outfielder for the California Angels. After his playing days were over, Darrell moved into the Angels' front office and is now the team's chief scout in Southern California and Arizona.

Tammy, the youngest, made her mark in volleyball, playing in college at California State–Fullerton. She is now studying to be a lawyer.

As for basketball stardom, that was left for Cheryl and Reggie. For many years, it was Cheryl who drew the most attention on the basketball court.

Talent runs in Reggie Miller's family. Miller demonstrates his talent on the basketball court, as he tries to swat the ball away from his opponent.

One of the reasons was that, for the first years of his life, Reggie could do little more than watch his older brothers and sister play. Reggie was born with some physical problems. Deformities in his legs and hips caused his feet to be turned completely inward. He wore braces that helped to turn his feet outward, but doctors still warned the family that he would never be able to walk normally. "Yes, he will," said a determined Carrie Miller. "I say he will."

Reggie was just as determined as his mother and eventually joined his siblings and other playmates in the driveway of the Miller home, where they shot the basketball toward the backboard and rim built over the garage.

Even though Reggie was now in the game, he was no match for his older sister. She clearly had a knack for the game and went on to a spectacular career in high school and college. In fact, Cheryl Miller is today widely regarded as the greatest women's basketball player in history. In 1995 she was elected to the Naismith Memorial Basketball Hall of Fame, one of the few women in the Hall.

For a while, Reggie's role on the court was to provide opposition for Cheryl in developing her game. Saul used Reggie as a defensive player to help Cheryl and her girlfriends work on their offensive skills.

Although he got a late start, Reggie quickly learned to play. The family had moved into a new home in Riverside, and Saul, Sr., carved out a section of hillside and poured concrete to create a small basketball court for his kids. Here Reggie began perfecting his deadly shooting touch. "My first goal was to master every shot in that area," said Reggie. When he achieved that, he asked his dad to expand the court. Saul kept putting down more concrete until it extended out twenty-three feet from the basket. That still wasn't enough to

Young Reggie perfected his incredible shooting on the concrete basketball court his father made for him in the Miller backyard.

satisfy Reggie, who kept stepping out farther until he was shooting from his mother's rose garden.

There were no basketball camps for any of the Miller kids. Saul, Sr., provided the instruction for Cheryl and Reggie. Even after he reached the National Basketball Association, Reggie returned to Riverside for two weeks every summer to work on his game with his dad. "I still see things in his game I can help him with," says Saul.

His father's influence is still evident in Reggie. Once, after a bad game in high school, Saul told Reggie that he hadn't played worth 50 cents. Reggie began taping two quarters under one of his wristbands to remind himself of that remark, a practice he continued even after reaching the NBA.

Early in his life, Reggie had a rather awkward shooting style. It wasn't until his sophomore year at Polytechnic High School that he began developing the smooth jump shot that has become his trademark. By that time, he had also grown as tall as Cheryl and was actually able to give her a battle in their backyard one-on-one matchups. It was when he was able to block one of her shots, swatting the ball off the court and into their mother's flower beds, that both Reggie and Cheryl knew the tide was turning.

But Cheryl was still the bigger star in high school, although their parents tried to pay equal attention to both of them. "We had a tradition," said Saul, Sr., "that at least one parent would be at every one of their games." Since the girls' and boys' games sometimes fell on the same night, Carrie and Saul would split up. Saul usually followed Cheryl, in part because he was a valued part of the Poly girls' team. "Cheryl had some problems with ankle sprains," he explained, "so I would come and tape her ankles before the game. The girls' team didn't have its own trainer, and pretty soon I was doing the taping for the entire team."

On the nights that Cheryl and Reggie both played, Saul and Carrie would come home from each game and fill one another in on how their children had done.

After one of Reggie's first games in high school, he and his mother came home with exciting news. Reggie had scored 39 points, an outstanding total. Then Saul arrived with the report from the girls' game. Cheryl had scored 105 points. She had also made two slam-dunk baskets and was credited with being the first female player ever to dunk a basketball in an organized game.

Some brothers may have felt deflated to have a fine performance overshadowed by their sister, but Carrie and Saul made sure that both felt good about their performances. "We were just as proud of Reggie's 39 points as we were of Cheryl's 105." As for Reggie, he was equally proud of his sister. To this day, he still ranks as one of his top basketball thrills the night his sister scored 105 points in a single game.

At times, Reggie and Cheryl would combine their talents. They had a favorite trick they loved to pull on the playgrounds of Riverside. Reggie would approach two young men on a court and ask, "You want to play my sister and me for five dollars?" The bet was too irresistible to pass up, and the Miller tandem would win easily. "We'd let them score the first five points and then make the bet double or nothing," said Reggie. Then Cheryl would start raining the jump shots. "Boom, boom, she'd shoot and we'd win, then be off to McDonald's with the money we won," said Reggie.

This kind of teamwork is typical of the relationship between Reggie and Cheryl Miller. There has never been any jealousy or rivalry between them. They have always been best friends and still are. In his Indiana home today, Reggie has a bedroom that is reserved just for Cheryl when she visits.

Cheryl Miller, Reggie's older sister, is considered by many to be the best women's basketball player of all time. Cheryl credits Reggie with teaching her the value of practice.

Cheryl feels just as strongly toward Reggie and is never shy about expressing how much her brother helped her. "I had no work ethic until Reggie taught me the value of practice," said Cheryl. "What people don't understand is that every point I scored was because of him."

Saul, Sr., says this indicates how close all the Millers were while growing up. "In our family, we have to help support each other, to help everyone improve. We believe Reggie made Cheryl and Cheryl made Reggie."

Reggie overcame early hardships to become a star, but he wasn't the only talented member of the family to do so. His older brother, Darrell, had eye problems early in his life and had to wear thick glasses by the time he was two years old. Just as Saul and Carrie were told that Reggie would probably never walk normally, they were also warned that Darrell would never do anything requiring coordination with his eyes. Despite that, Darrell went on to a career in major-league baseball and often played catcher, one of the most difficult defensive positions.

The family also had an early scare with Cheryl, who nearly suffocated at birth because the umbilical cord ended up wrapped around her neck.

Their father says they are a spiritual family and that their faith helped in overcoming barriers. "God had a plan for these kids," he said, "and that plan would not be interrupted."

Chapter 3

When it came time to pick a college to attend, both Cheryl and Reggie Miller had more than their share to choose from. Cheryl, being a year older, went first and settled on the University of Southern California (USC), located in the heart of Los Angeles.

She quickly became the star of the USC women's basketball team. The Lady Trojans won the NCAA women's national championship in 1983 and 1984, Cheryl's first two years on the team. Cheryl was named to the All-American team in each of her four seasons at USC. She was also a member of the 1984 United States Olympic team that won a gold medal in women's basketball.

Cheryl was a tough act for anyone to follow, let alone a younger brother who was trying to make a name for himself, but Reggie attracted a lot of attention from college recruiters because of his skills. He eventually selected a college with a great basketball tradition, the University of California–Los Angeles (UCLA). It wasn't just basketball that interested him about the school, however. Reggie Miller's original major was drama, and he was attracted to UCLA's theater department. In fact, it was a phone call from a notable UCLA graduate that helped to finalize Reggie's decision. The call came from Mike Warren, who was a member of two UCLA national championship teams in the 1960s. Warren went on to fame as Officer Bobby Hill on the television show *Hill Street Blues.*

Even though he was at a different college, Reggie Miller was still hounded by comparisons to his famous sister. Early in his college career, a *Sports Illustrated* article on the UCLA Bruins made the statement that, "[Reggie] Miller has the distinction of being the first Bruin who can't outplay his sister."

But Miller had other shadows to contend with, as did anyone else going to UCLA to play basketball. Championship banners adorn Pauley Pavilion, the Bruins' home. UCLA won ten national titles under legendary coach John Wooden in the 1960s and 1970s. Lew Alcindor (who later changed his name to Kareem Abdul-Jabbar), the greatest college basketball player ever, led the Bruins to three of those championships.

Even Miller's first coach at UCLA, Larry Farmer, was a reminder of those glory days. Larry Farmer had played on three of Wooden's championship teams in the early 1970s. As a coach, Farmer preferred upperclassmen to freshmen like Miller. Not only that, Miller—who played forward in college—was the backup for one of the team's best players, Kenny Fields.

But Miller still played in all twenty-eight of the Bruins' games in 1983–84, even though he didn't start any of them. When he did get off the bench, he made the most of the chance. Coach Farmer was not fond of the type of long-range shooting Reggie Miller was known for, but Miller was careful in his shot selection and made more than 50 percent of his field goal attempts over the course of the season. Miller

Though Reggie Miller played in all twenty-eight of UCLA's games during his freshman year, he didn't start in any of them.

averaged 4.9 points per game and was named the Bruins' most valuable freshman player.

Reggie Miller had a new coach to play for in his sophomore season, as Walt Hazzard, another former great player for the Bruins, replaced Farmer. Hazzard first played in the NBA with the Los Angeles Lakers and he was still friends with some current members of the team. As a result, several of them would work out at Pauley Pavilion over the summer. Byron Scott, Michael Cooper, and Earvin "Magic" Johnson were among the Lakers who would stop by and play in pickup games with some of the UCLA players who happened to be practicing there at the time.

Reggie Miller benefitted greatly from the presence of the Lakers in those workouts. "Byron, Magic, and Cooper took me under their wings and told me that I had what it took to make it in the NBA," Miller recalled years later. "They just told me to watch, listen, and learn." And he did.

Reggie Miller was ready to play a greater role for UCLA his sophomore season. Kenny Fields was gone, having completed his college eligibility. This opened up a spot in the starting lineup.

Reggie Miller started the Bruins' first six games of the season, averaging 12.7 points per game. Hazzard liked Miller's ability to score from the outside and, unlike Farmer, didn't mind watching Miller put up a long jump shot. College basketball had not yet adopted the three-point rule for shots taken beyond a certain distance. If it had been in effect, there's no question that Reggie Miller's point totals would have been even higher. For the most part, things were looking up for Reggie Miller.

There were a couple of problems, though. Hazzard wanted to see Miller pulling down more rebounds than the two per game he was grabbing. Also, Miller lost control of his temper in the team's sixth game, against Brigham Young University. He got into a minor fight with BYU's Timo Saarelainen that ended up with the two players spitting at one another.

Miller was embarrassed about the incident and apologized publicly. Hazzard also didn't start Miller in the team's next game as punishment for his behavior. This game, against St. John's University at Madison Square Garden in New York, turned out to be a turning point for Reggie Miller and UCLA.

The Bruins were outplayed by St. John's, 88–69, and Hazzard was angry. He accused his players of quitting in the game, which had been shown on national television. Hazzard was especially disappointed by the lack of effort of some of his upperclassmen. After the game, he indicated that he would start giving younger players more playing time.

UCLA was not playing well under their new coach, losing five of their first seven games, and Hazzard was ready to shake things up. Reggie Miller had played very little in the St. John's game, but he was back in the starting lineup in the team's next game, scoring 14 points in a win against Oral Roberts University. Reggie Miller played consistently from then on, usually finishing with point totals in double figures. He also picked up the pace in rebounding and went on to double his rebounding average.

The Bruins as a team also started playing better. They lost their Pacific 10 conference opener at Oregon State, but then went on a roll. They won thirteen of their next nineteen games, with the six games they lost being close ones. All the losses were either in overtime or by one point.

Reggie Miller played a leading role in the team's surge and was spending little time on the bench. During the conference season, he averaged 39 out of a possible 42.5 minutes per game. In fact, during a four-overtime contest

A change in coaches and added experience allowed Reggie Miller more playing time in his sophomore year. In fact, he averaged 39 out of a possible 42.5 minutes per game in the regular season.

against the University of Southern California, Reggie Miller played all but one minute of the sixty-minute game.

Miller went on to lead the team with an average of 15.2 points per game. He became the first sophomore to lead UCLA in scoring since the great Bill Walton had accomplished the same feat in 1972.

With a record of 16 wins and 12 losses, the Bruins received a bid in the National Invitational Tournament (NIT). UCLA cruised to wins over Montana and Nebraska in the tournament's first two games with Reggie Miller totalling 60 points for the two games. UCLA then turned on the defense, holding Fresno State to 43 points and beating them by ten points. This advanced the Bruins to the tournament Final Four at Madison Square Garden in New York.

Hazzard remembered the humiliating loss to St. John's the last time UCLA had played at Madison Square Garden. He was thrilled to have the chance to return to New York and erase memories of that game. "We're going to show the world the new Bruins, the real Bruins," he said confidently.

The Bruins semifinal game was against the Louisville Cardinals, a team they had beaten easily during the regular season; but this time the Cardinals proved to be a tougher opponent. Reggie Miller missed his first two shots, both from long range, and came out of the game. Some thought Hazzard was benching him for not taking good shots. As it turned out, it was an equipment problem. Miller's athletic supporter had broken, and he had to put on a new one. His coach had just as much confidence in his star sophomore as ever.

Back in the game, Reggie Miller racked up ten points through the remainder of the first half, giving UCLA a 36–33 lead at halftime. The Bruins went on to a 75–66 win to advance to the tournament championship game against the Indiana Hoosiers.

Like UCLA, Indiana had a hot-shooting sophomore in Steve Alford.

Both Miller and Alford played well in the title game. Indiana got off to an early lead and led by as much as six points in the first half. But UCLA closed the gap and tied the game, 29–29, on Miller's jumper from the right side just before halftime.

In the second half, the Hoosiers again got off to a quick start, opening up a 35–31 lead. But then it was time for Reggie Miller to get hot. He scored ten points in a hurry and the Bruins took command.

Indiana made a late run and pulled to within two points after a basket by Alford, but Miller answered with a field goal of his own to pad the Bruins' lead. UCLA won the game, 65–62, and Reggie Miller was named the Most Valuable Player (MVP) for the entire tournament.

In accepting the award, Miller acknowledged two of his teammates, Brad Wright and Nigel Miguel, who had also played well. "The MVP could have gone to Nigel or Brad Wright. But I'm glad it came to me. This is really sweet. We and the coach took a lot of verbal abuse."

Hazzard referred to that abuse in his comments after the game: "Newspapers and magazines said we couldn't play. But here we are. We won the championship, and the Most Valuable Player is a sophomore. A magazine article said Reggie couldn't beat his sister one-on-one. I wish the writer would put some salt and pepper on it and eat that article."

Although the NIT championship would be the high point of Miller's college career, he did have two more good seasons with UCLA. During his junior season, he averaged 27.8 points in conference play. That set a new Pacific 10 record. One of the players who had held the old record was Lew Alcindor. Near the end of the season, Reggie Miller scored 41 points

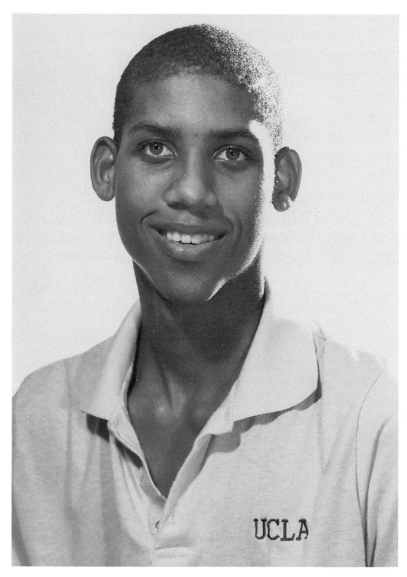

Reggie Miller was named Most Valuable Player of the the National Invitational Tournament after the Bruins beat the Hoosiers, 65–62, in the Tournament finals.

against Oregon State, his best college game ever. It was the fifth time that season that he scored 35 or more points.

Miller also stood out during the year because of his fine free-throw shooting. He made more than 88 percent of the free throws he tried, one of the top percentages in the nation.

The three-point field goal was finally added to college basketball in 1986, and Reggie Miller took advantage of it. He connected on nearly 44 percent of his three-point shots, an outstanding total. By the time his college career was over, he had scored more than 2,000 points. Only two Bruins, Lew Alcindor being one of them, had ever scored more for UCLA.

The comparions to his sister would still be made, but Reggie was making a name for himself, and even his sister was finding that out. Cheryl once tried to get into an exclusive Los Angeles nightclub. The fact that she was the greatest women's basketball player ever didn't mean anything to the door attendant, but then she came up with the magic words that got her ushered in: "I'm Reggie Miller's sister."

Chapter 4

After four years at UCLA, Reggie Miller was ready for the big time—the National Basketball Association. He was one of the top players coming out of college in 1987, and a lot of teams were hoping to have the chance to pick him in the NBA's draft of college players. Magic Johnson and a few of the other Lakers who worked out in the summer at UCLA were well aware of how good Reggie Miller was. Johnson even put in a good word with the Lakers' management on behalf of Miller.

It wasn't that the Lakers weren't interested in Reggie Miller, but they had just won the NBA championship. As a result, they would have the last pick in the draft. Miller was too good to be available that long. In fact, he was the 11th player picked. He was selected by the Indiana Pacers.

The draft pick wasn't popular in Indiana, where the fans had hoped the Pacers would take Steve Alford, the great star from Indiana University. They were upset when the Pacers passed on Alford, and they refused to support any other player that was drafted. In the case of Reggie Miller, it may have been even worse. Indiana fans remembered that it was Miller who helped UCLA beat Alford and the Indiana Hoosiers in the 1985 National Invitational Tournament.

Some Pacers fans were so upset that they even cancelled their season tickets. It was a tough situation for a young player to be going into. Miller, however, didn't seem fazed by it and said the fans of Indiana would come to accept him once they saw him play.

He was right. It didn't take long before the fans figured out that the Pacers did the right thing in drafting Miller instead of Alford. Alford never fit into the NBA and didn't last long in the league. Meanwhile, Reggie Miller quickly showed that he was going to have an outstanding career.

Miller would be playing a new position in the pros. He had been a forward in high school and college. At six feet seven inches, Reggie Miller was at an in-between height for the NBA—too tall to be a guard but too short to be a forward. Some players like Miller end up playing both forward and guard, but the Pacers wanted Miller to concentrate on one position and put him in the backcourt.

Reggie Miller quickly won over the Indiana fans with his exciting style of play. He averaged ten points per game his rookie season while playing in all eighty two Indiana games. From three-point range, he connected on 35 percent of his attempts.

His ability to shoot the three-point basket thrilled the crowd. It also made things easier for his teammates. Opponents had to keep an eye on Miller out near the three-point line. This opened up the area around the basket and helped Indiana's inside game.

Reggie Miller had more in his arsenal than just a deadly shooting eye from the outside. He could drive the lane and put

Many fans who expected the Pacers to pick Indiana University star Steve Alford in the draft were surprised when Reggie Miller was chosen instead. Miller's exciting style of play soon won over the skeptical Pacers' fans.

up a one-handed shot while seeming to float in the air. He was also skilled at starting fast breaks for his team.

He played hard, but at the same time made it clear he was having fun. In his first three years in the league, Reggie Miller steadily increased the amount of time he was playing and the number of points he was scoring. He averaged 24.6 points per game in 1989–90, a career-high for him. He also made the Eastern Conference All-Star team for the first time. He made two of the three shots he tried in the All-Star Game, scoring four points in fourteen minutes of play.

Reggie Miller was a threat from the outside, sinking 150 three-point baskets, but he could also move into traffic and score—or at least draw a foul. Since he had developed into one of the best free-throw shooters in the league, his ability to get to the free-throw line was important.

He had the highest NBA free-throw percentage in 1990–91, sinking 91.8 percent of his shots from the line. Throughout his career, he has averaged well over 85 percent in his free-throw shooting. One NBA coach saw this as one of Reggie's greatest strengths. "That's a part of the game that's underrated, getting to the line, especially when you're as good a foul shooter as Miller is."

The Pacers play in the NBA's Central Division, along with the Chicago Bulls. This meant that Reggie Miller would have plenty of chances to match up against Chicago's Michael Jordan, perhaps the greatest basketball player ever.

Through the years, the two have had some memorable meetings; Reggie Miller remembers them well, as does Michael Jordan. "I love challenges," Miller has said, "and playing against Michael is the biggest chess match in the world." It's also one that has taught Reggie Miller a few lessons.

It was during a pre-season game in 1988 that Reggie Miller held his own against the great Chicago star for three quarters. Then Chuck Person, Miller's teammate, suggested that he try to intimidate Jordan with a little trash talk. Miller quickly learned that this was not the right strategy to try with someone like Michael Jordan.

Instead of backing down, Jordan stepped up. As Miller tried feebly to guard him, Jordan scored twenty points in the fourth quarter. As the game ended and the players were leaving the court, Jordan walked by Miller and said, "Don't you ever talk mess with me again."

Reggie Miller looked down and thought, "You are absolutely right, *Mister* Jordan."

But there would be more chances for Reggie Miller to prove himself against Jordan. The Bulls and Pacers met at Market Square Arena in Indianapolis in January of 1990. Miller hit his first four field-goal attempts of the game, three of them being three-pointers. "After that, I felt I couldn't miss," Miller said later. "My teammates sensed this aura of indestructibility and began looking for me."

Reggie Miller scored thirteen points in just the first quarter. However, Jordan had nine points himself and the game was tied, 30–30. Miller laid back in the second quarter, letting his teammates carry the scoring load, which they did. Indiana led 65–49 at the half.

In the locker room, Chuck Person told Miller to start shooting more in the second half. Miller did, scoring twelve points in the third quarter, then reeling off the Pacers' first eight points of the final period.

Jordan hung with Miller for awhile and helped his team pull to within four points late in the game; but Indiana ended up winning, 120–113. Jordan had 35 points, a fine game, but the spotlight was on Reggie Miller, who ended up with 44 points. "What made it special and memorable was that all those points came against Michael Jordan," Reggie said.

Reggie Miller outscored Michael Jordan by nine points in a game against the Chicago Bulls in January 1990.

"He tried everything to stop me, but he couldn't. It was just one of those nights."

When this night ended, Jordan came up to Reggie Miller and shook his hand. But while congratulating him, Jordan added, "I'll be back."

Miller nodded and said, "I know."

Jordan and Miller have battled one another fiercely on the court. Sometimes it reached the point where neither could control his temper. In a game in early 1993, Miller tipped in a missed shot by teammate Pooh Richardson in the first quarter. As Miller turned to run back downcourt, he bumped Jordan with his forearm. Jordan chased Miller down and the two began fighting. Reggie Miller ended up being ejected from the game. Jordan, who was not, went on to score 40 points.

Miller was upset about the incident. He felt Jordan had received preferential treatment from the referees because he was such a great player. The National Basketball Association agreed after viewing the films of the game. The league suspended Jordan for one game and made it clear that Jordan was the instigator in the fight. Despite their battles, however, Miller and Jordan developed great respect for one another.

For a while, however, Michael Jordan and the Bulls would become less significant to Reggie Miller and the Pacers. In 1993, the Pacers focused on the New York Knicks, their opponents in the first round of the playoffs. Although Miller averaged over 31 points a game in the series, the Knicks ended up winning the best-of-five series, three games to one.

Then in October of that year, just a few weeks before the opening of the NBA season, Michael Jordan announced he was retiring from the game. (After pursuing a career in professional baseball, Jordan eventually returned to the Bulls in March of 1995.)

The loss of Jordan was obviously a blow to the Chicago

Bulls. However, it opened up the Central Division, and the Pacers were one of the teams to take advantage of that. Indiana had a new coach, Larry Brown, but it took them a while to get going in the 1993–94 season. Brown made it clear he would be relying on Reggie Miller to lead the team. At the same time, the new coach said Miller would have to do more than just score to be the team leader. "Larry made it clear to Reggie that he wanted him to play an all-around game and not just be a scorer," said Pacers' president Donnie Walsh. "And Reggie responded."

The Pacers came together in the second half of the 1993–94 season, winning thirty-one of their last forty-three games. They were on a roll going into the playoffs and continued to rumble in the opening rounds. They polished off Shaquille O'Neal and the Orlando Magic in three straight games, then defeated the Atlanta Hawks, the team with the best regular-season record in the Eastern Conference.

They would again play the New York Knicks, the team that had eliminated them from the playoffs the year before. It was in this series that Reggie Miller had his big performance, scoring twenty-five points in the fourth quarter of Game Five. However, the best-of-seven series still ended up in disappointment for Indiana. The Knicks won the last two games to beat the Pacers, four games to three.

Reggie Miller still had a new challenge to look forward to in the summer of 1994. He was selected to play on the United States team in the World Basketball Championships to be played in Toronto, Ontario, Canada.

Back in 1992, Reggie Miller had come close to making the United States Olympic basketball team, known as the "Dream Team." It was the first time the United States had used professionals on the squad. With Magic Johnson, David Robinson, Larry Bird, Michael Jordan, and

Patrick Ewing, the United States had little trouble winning the gold medal.

The United States squad for the 1994 World Championships became known as "Dream Team II." Reggie Miller's teammates included Shaquille O'Neal, Larry Johnson, Alonzo Mourning, and Dominique Wilkins. Dream Team II had little trouble with any of its opponents. Reggie Miller ended up as the second-leading scorer on the team, averaging 17.1 points in the eight-game tournament. In the second half of a game against Australia, Miller scored twenty-three points. Then, against Puerto Rico in the first half of their next game, he hit eight three-point shots and scored twenty-six points. In two halves of a game, Reggie Miller had scored 49 points.

Even though the squad was loaded with talent, Reggie Miller was called "the most compelling member of the United States team" by Harvey Araton of *The New York Times.*

Participating on Dream Team II was a good tune-up for the 1994–95 season. Reggie Miller helped lead the Pacers to the Central Division title.

The year before they had advanced to the Eastern Conference championship round. In 1995, the team would be satisfied with nothing less than an NBA title. In the first round of the playoffs, they swept the three-game series against the Atlanta Hawks. Reggie Miller averaged 31 points per game in the series, over ten points more than he averaged during the regular season. "Like most great players, Reggie seems to get better as the stakes get higher," team president Donnie Walsh has said in the past. Reggie Miller's playoff performance showed that to be the case.

The Pacers' next opponent would be the winner of the series between the Cleveland Cavaliers and the New York Knicks. That series was not yet finished by the time Indiana had finished off Atlanta.

Playing in the Olympics helped Reggie Miller warm up for the 1994–95 season. He led the Pacers to the Central Division title.

Miller was asked whether he would rather play the Knicks or the Cavaliers. He thought back over the last two years, when the Knicks had eliminated the Pacers each time in the playoffs.

"We have some ghosts to exorcise," he replied. "If you leave it up to me, I'd like to play the Knicks."

Two days later, the Knicks beat the Cavaliers to capture their playoff series and advance to the next round against the Pacers.

Reggie Miller got his wish.

Chapter 5

"My theory on shots when I'm all alone is that I should make 70 percent of them," Reggie Miller has said. "I don't think other players set standards that high. That's a mistake."

Miller's feelings are revealing. Making a basket when he's left alone—or open on the court—is the easy part. Getting open is the hard part.

Once open, Reggie Miller has shown himself to be as good a shooter as anyone in basketball. "Shooting is concentration and rhythm," he says, "and sometimes it is pure confidence. Sometimes things are going so right you feel you can will the ball into the basket."

Things were going right for Reggie Miller during the incredible quarter in which he scored 25 points against the Knicks in June of 1993. Typically, five of his baskets during that run were from three-point range. As much as anyone who ever played the game, Reggie Miller has taken advantage of the three-point basket.

During the 1994–95 regular season, Miller set an Indiana team record with 195 three-point baskets, giving him more than 1,000 in his career. In addition, he became the first player in NBA history to make at least 100 three-pointers per season in six straight seasons.

Despite his ability to make this productive shot, Miller normally doesn't go out of his way to shoot it. If he gets the ball and has a good look at the basket, he'll put it up from wherever he is. Unlike some players, he rarely makes a point of stepping back behind the three-point line before he shoots. "I never want to be conscious of the line," he says. "I never get ticked off, like some guys do, if my foot's on the line and I get a two [-point basket] instead of a three. It's too difficult just to get open. My eyes are looking ahead of me, to the point where I'm going to get the pass and take my shot, so they can't be looking down at the floor."

While he doesn't get hung up on it, Reggie Miller does take pride in being such a great three-point shooter. In fact, Miller was one of the players who was unhappy when the NBA decided to move the line to shorten the distance needed for a three-point basket. "It geeks me off that they moved the line in," he said. When asked why, Miller explained, "Now everyone will be able to do it."

But for Reggie Miller, the bigger battle comes down to shaking off an opposing team's guard to get that open shot. With curls and cuts, sprints and slashes, he does whatever is necessary to find himself alone with the ball. He may dart behind his own players who have positioned themselves to block out defenders, or he may have to shake off the opposition himself.

George Irvine, a Pacers assistant coach, said that once Reggie Miller gets the ball, it's usually too late to stop him. "Most teams' strategy in stopping Reggie is to beat him up before he gets the ball," Irvine explains.

As someone who has always prided himself on taking long shots from the outside, Miller was upset that the NBA decided to shorten the distance between the three-point line and the basket.

Basketball can be a rough game, and Reggie Miller takes his share of jolts while running through an obstacle course to find a good spot to shoot from. But Miller enjoys this part of the game—the on-the-floor combat—as much as anything.

His clashes with opposing players—both physically and mentally—are something Miller enjoys. During the 1993 playoffs between Indiana and New York, Reggie Miller engaged in some "mind games" with John Starks, the Knick who was guarding him. Miller's trash talking achieved its purpose. He frustrated his opponent so much that Starks finally butted Miller in the face with his head. Starks was ejected from the game; Miller had won the battle.

Because of his mouth, his style, and his ability, Reggie Miller is like a lightning rod for the booing of fans in opposing arenas. Almost anything he does is taken as a sign of hot-dogging. As part of his follow-through after a shot, Miller often keeps his right arm extended in the air. "I do it because when my father taught me to shoot, he taught me to extend that arm and keep it up there real high." Often, though, it is interpreted as a taunting gesture by his opponents and their fans.

That fact has not escaped Reggie Miller. As a result, he may even make a point of leaving his arm in the air just a shade longer. He doesn't mind the boos he hears on the road. In some ways, he welcomes them. "I like being the bad guy," he has said. "I wish I could play all my games on the road."

Reggie Miller says some of this goes back to his childhood when he would watch movies and root for the villain. Miller likes playing the role of villain so much that sometimes he feels like he's on stage. Once, after scoring a key basket against the Bulls in Chicago, he riled the crowd further by turning and bowing to them.

"When it comes to getting under people's skin, nobody can touch him," said Derek Harper of the New York Knicks.

Miller even had the chance to strut his style on the big screen in 1995. He had a couple of brief appearances playing himself in the movie *Forget Paris*. Miller did a little trash talking with opponents and traded insults with a basketball referee played by comedian Billy Crystal.

Reggie Miller says there's a reason for his trash talk other than to irritate opponents. "I think trash talking jacks me up. It gives me security. I know I'm not the best. I'm lucky to be here. So a lot of times on the court I'll talk to myself to motivate myself."

Even off the court, Reggie Miller has found ways to raise eyebrows. Hardly anyone thought that the United States team that played in the World Championships in the summer of 1994 had the talent of the 1992 U.S. Olympic team. But Reggie Miller did and upset even a few of the veterans of the original Dream Team when he said that he and his Dream Team II teammates would have had no trouble beating them.

Sometimes he seems to go out of his way to attract attention, but Miller hints at the fact that this kind of behavior doesn't really describe him. "I don't want people to know me," he says. "The less you know about someone, the more mysterious he is. That's what makes Michael Jackson so famous."

The president of the Pacers, Donnie Walsh, says he knows the real Reggie Miller, who is much different than the image he likes to project. "Reggie's public persona is the opposite of what he really is," says Walsh, who remembers a brash image Reggie tried to project on a television interview. "After that, I was in a restaurant trying to tell a writer that Reggie's not like that. Then Reggie walks in with two ball boys he's taking out to dinner, and I said, 'That's the Reggie I know.'"

Although Miller projects a tough image on the court, he has shown a much softer side off the court. He has been known to take ball boys out to dinner and visit sick children in hospitals.

Reggie Miller loves being around young people and cares a great deal about them. He has hosted a cable television talk show for teenagers, which was videotaped at the Children's Museum of Indianapolis. Miller has also been active in supporting the United Negro College Fund.

He also hasn't forgotten some of his early struggles, when he had to wear braces to correct the deformities in his legs. "I understand what it's like for a kid to be trapped inside behind four walls," he says. Keeping that in mind, Miller spends a lot of time visiting children in hospitals. He knows he can't cure their ills, but he can make their day a little brighter.

In a way, Reggie Miller's concern and affection for young people shows some of the innocent childlike qualities that he often likes to hide. His favorite movies are ones about teenagers, such as *Sixteen Candles* and *Pretty in Pink.*

Reggie Miller was raised in Southern California but is comfortable with the simpler life of the Midwest. In 1991, he signed a long-term contract with the Pacers that ensured he would stay in Indiana for many years to come.

Miller's wife, Marita Starvou-Miller, is a model who travels across the country for photo sessions. As a professional athlete, Miller does the same type of coast-to-coast travel, but he's always ready to settle back in his five-bedroom Indiana home and do something less glamorous: watch television, shoot pool, or read a book.

Chapter 6

Reggie Miller's big sister had one of her greatest moments in May of 1995. She was inducted into the Basketball Hall of Fame, one of the few females ever to receive this honor. Normally, Miller wouldn't have missed such an event, but this time, he couldn't get away. The Pacers were in the midst of their playoff series with the New York Knicks. For once, Cheryl was the one having trouble staying in the spotlight, considering the highlights her kid brother was unreeling.

The Pacers' 1995 playoff run featured a number of games with heartstopping finishes. Some went Indiana's way, others did not, but none could top the final seconds of the series opener against New York.

The first game was in Madison Square Garden, where Miller and the Pacers had been through their share of highs and lows. It looked like this one would be a low; the Knicks were clearly in control in the game's final minutes.

The Knicks were ahead, 97–93, when Miller stepped to the line for a pair of free throws. His nemesis, Spike Lee, started leading the fans behind the basket in waving their arms to distract Miller. It didn't work. He made his first shot, directed a glare toward Lee, then calmly made the other one.

The Knicks opened the gap back up to four points. Miller countered with a layup with a minute to go. It looked like Miller's late efforts wouldn't be enough, though. New York held a 105–99 edge as the Pacers called a time-out with just 18.7 seconds left on the clock.

When play resumed, Reggie Miller took the inbound pass on the left wing and fired a shot from three-point range. It swished through the net to make the score 105–102. Miller started downcourt but hustled back when he saw that Anthony Mason of the Knicks was having trouble inbounding the ball from under the basket. Miller collided with New York's Greg Anthony, who fell to the floor as Mason released his pass. Miller intercepted the ball and dribbled back to behind the three-point line. From almost the same spot he had launched his last shot, Reggie let another one fly. The shot was good.

In just over three seconds, Reggie Miller had scored six points to tie the game. But he wasn't done yet. After John Starks of the Knicks missed two free throws and Patrick Ewing couldn't connect on a follow-up jumper, Miller grabbed the rebound and was fouled by Mason. With 7.5 seconds remaining, Reggie Miller stepped to the line. He had already made twelve of thirteen free throws, and he wasn't about to miss now. He made both and the Pacers had pulled out an incredible 107–105 victory.

The Knicks and their fans were stunned. It had looked like a sure win for them, but Reggie Miller—almost singlehandedly—had stolen it away from them.

Even Pacers' coach Larry Brown had trouble believing what he had just seen. "Realistically, I thought we had no chance," he said later. "I couldn't imagine us coming back. But until it's over, you've got to keep trying."

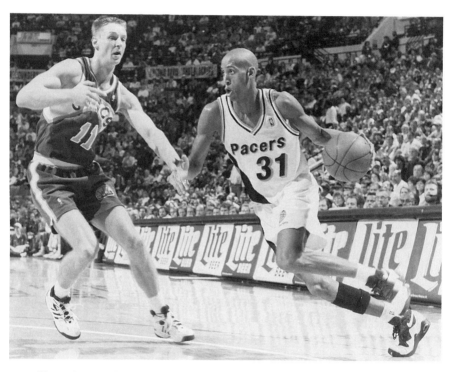

Shown here against the SuperSonics, Reggie Miller also led the Pacers to an incredible come-from-behind victory in the playoff series opener against the Knicks.

As the Pacers ran off the court, Reggie Miller looked back and hollered at the Knicks, "Choke artists." He also said in a post-game interview that, "We think we can sweep this team."

But the Pacers were still in for a great battle. The Knicks won the second game and play shifted to Indiana.

In Game Three, Miller changed his methods. He didn't sink a single three-pointer and did most of his scoring from inside. He also plucked rebounds at a greater than usual pace. The lead shifted back and forth between the Knicks and Pacers early in the game. It stayed close in the second quarter, but the Knicks were starting to open up a lead as the half ended.

Indiana found itself behind, 87–76 in the fourth quarter. At that point, they started to mount a comeback. They cut the gap to eight points. Miller then sank two free throws to bring them closer. The next time downcourt, he drove into the lane, banking home a shot as he was falling. With 45 seconds left in regulation time, Miller drove in again, this time with a chance to tie the game. He missed, but ten seconds later teammate Rik Smits scored to make it an 88–88 game. The score was still tied as the final seconds ticked off. Miller put up a three-pointer as the buzzer sounded, but the ball bounced off the rim and the game went into overtime.

In the overtime period, Reggie Miller grabbed three rebounds—giving him 11 for the game—which helped the Pacers open up a 94–90 lead. With 41 seconds left, Miller cut to the basket, took a pass, and dunked the ball. He finished the game with 26 points, as Indiana held on for a 97–95 win.

Indiana won again in Game Four and was within one victory of winning the best-of-seven series. The next game would be back in New York. Reggie Miller wanted nothing more than to finish off the Knicks in Madison Square Garden. It looked like the Pacers would do just that even though they trailed by five points late in the game.

Reggie Miller tried a three-pointer that missed with less than a minute to play. He got another shot a few seconds later and connected on a thirty-footer to close to within two points. Then, with 5 seconds to go, Byron Scott sank another three-pointer to give the Pacers a 95–94 lead. The Knicks weren't dead yet, though. Patrick Ewing took a pass, spun into the lane, and scored, to put the Knicks up by a point with 1.8 seconds left.

Indiana called time out and then inbounded the ball from midcourt. It was Reggie Miller they wanted taking the shot. The Knicks knew that and kept him covered. Miller cut through traffic and took the pass. With a defender in his face, he let loose with a three-pointer that could win the game. But it wasn't to be. The shot missed and the Knicks won the game to stay alive in the series.

When the Knicks won the sixth game, as well, the series was tied. Miller knew it would be the Pacers who would be labeled as "choke artists" if they lost this series now. Game Seven would be in New York, right where Reggie Miller wanted the Knicks. He'd have another chance to beat them on their home court.

Miller was hot early, scoring eighteen points through the first two quarters. Indiana led by four at halftime and started to pull away in the third quarter. Miller sank a three-pointer to make the score 71–59. Then he buried another and the lead was fifteen. The Knicks surged back and even took a one-point lead midway through the final quarter. The teams battled through the final minutes. Indiana clung to a 97–95 lead with five seconds left, but it was the Knicks' ball. Once again they went to their big center, Patrick Ewing, who drove into the lane. His shot bounced off the back of the rim as the buzzer sounded to end the game.

The Pacers found themselves battling with the Knicks once again in the 1995 playoffs.

As Indiana celebrated, Reggie Miller dropped to his knees, pressed his head against the floor, and said, "Finally."

Not only had they finally beaten the Knicks, the Pacers were back in the Eastern Conference Finals for the second-straight year. Their opponents would be the Orlando Magic, led by center Shaquille O'Neal and point guard Anfernee Hardaway.

Playing at home, Orlando won the first two games. The Pacers came back with a 105–100 win as Miller scored 26 points. They then tried to tie up the series in Game Four, which went right down to the wire. Indiana led 89–87 when Brian Shaw of the Magic sank a three-pointer with 13.3 seconds left. But Reggie Miller answered with a three-pointer of his own. It put the Pacers back out in front, 92–90, with 5.2 seconds showing on the clock. Orlando wasn't done, though. Hardaway took the inbound pass and hit another three-point basket. The Magic were up by a point with just 1.3 seconds left.

After taking a time out, the Pacers were able to inbound from midcourt. As usual, they hoped to get the ball to Reggie Miller, but the Magic kept him covered as he tried to squirm away. Instead the inbound pass went to Rik Smits. Smits pumped, ducked under Tree Rollins of the Magic, and fired a game-winning shot as time expired.

The Pacers had come back to win the game. In doing so, they had come back to tie the best-of-seven series at two games each.

They came back again in the fifth game, although it wasn't enough. Down by fourteen points with just over four minutes to play, the Pacers reeled off ten-straight points. They still fell short, though, losing the game, 108–106.

Another comeback was needed. The Pacers came out shooting in Game Six. Reggie Miller was on fire as he scored twenty points in the opening quarter. He upped his point total to twenty-eight as Indiana built a twenty-five-point lead at halftime.

The Pacers increased the lead to as much as thirty-five points and cruised to a 123–96 win, once again tying up the series. Reggie Miller finished with 36 points. Through the first six games, he was averaging 32 points a game.

The Pacers and the Magic would meet in a seventh and final game in Orlando with the winner advancing to the NBA Finals. "Game Seven's the best," said Reggie Miller. "It's what I live for."

With a quick start, Orlando got off to a twelve-point lead, but the Pacers came back to cut the margin to three points at the end of one quarter. Indiana trailed, 52–45, at halftime but was still in the game. Reggie Miller had just seven points in the first half, and Brown indicated that he wanted his star to get some better shot opportunities. But the Orlando defense was tough. They fought through screens that Miller's teammates were setting and kept him covered. Meanwhile, the high-powered Orlando offense stayed hot. The Magic had a 73–55 lead with 4:44 left in the third quarter.

There was still time left for the Pacers. This time, though, they were out of comebacks. Orlando continued to pull away and finished with a 105–81 victory to reach the NBA finals.

The season was over for Reggie and the Pacers. It was a great season, even though none of them felt that way at the time. But only one team a year gets to finish its season without disappointment.

The Pacers stayed determined and would have to try again with Reggie Miller leading the way. Miller continued his consistent play in the 1995-96 season. His scoring average stayed around 20 points per game. It seemed that he could be counted on game after game to approach that total. And, as always, he could explode for a big night as he did January 23, 1996 when he scored 40 points in a 117-102 win over the Phoenix Suns. Miller made 12 of the 16 shots he took from the floor, including 6 three-point baskets.

The Pacers were a good team, but they knew they would have to get by other good teams to get what they wanted—an NBA championship.

The Chicago Bulls would be tough to beat now that Michael Jordan was back in basketball. The Orlando Magic had also shown that they were not a team to be overlooked.

And then, as Reggie Miller well knew, there were always the New York Knicks.

Career Statistics

Year	G	Min.	FGM	FGA	Pct.	FTM	FTA	Pct.	Reb.	Pts.	Pts. Avg.
1987–88	82	1,840	306	627	.488	149	186	.801	190	822	10.0
1988–89	74	2,536	398	831	.479	287	340	.844	292	1,181	16.0
1989–90	82	3,192	661	1,287	.514	544	627	.868	295	2,016	24.6
1990–91	82	2,972	596	1,164	.512	551	600	.918	281	1,855	22.6
1991–92	82	3,120	562	1,121	.501	442	515	.858	318	1,695	20.7
1992–93	82	2,954	571	1,193	.479	427	485	.880	258	1,736	21.2
1993–94	79	2,638	524	1,042	.503	403	444	.908	212	1,574	19.9
1994–95	81	2,665	505	1,092	.462	383	427	.897	210	1,588	19.6
TOTALS	644	21,917	4,123	8,357	.493	3,186	3,624	.879	2,056	12,467	19.4

G–Games Played

Min.–Minutes Played

FGM–Field Goals Made

FGA–Field Goals Attempted

FTM–Free Throws Made

FTA–Free Throws Attempted

Pct.–Percentage Made

Reb.–Rebounds

Pts.–Points Scored

Pts. Avg.–Average Points Per Game

Where to Write Reggie Miller:

Mr. Reggie Miller
Indiana Pacers
Market Square Arena
300 E. Market Street
Indianapolis, IN 46204

Index